Until Stones Blossom

Averil Meehan

SUMMER PALACE PRESS

First published in 2006 by

Summer Palace Press
Cladnageeragh, Kilbeg, Kilcar, County Donegal, Ireland

Printed by Nicholson & Bass Ltd.

A catalogue record for this book is available
from the British Library

ISBN 0 9552122 4 3

This book is printed on elemental chlorine-free paper

in memory of my parents,
Selma and Robert

Acknowledgments

Some of the poems in this book have previously appeared in: *Beyond the Rubicon* (Covehill Press 1999); *Eleven Ways to Kiss the Ground* (CD, Errigal Writers, 2001); *The Stinging Fly* and *Cork Literary Review*. Other poems have also been published in *Cyphers, Fingerpost, Full Moon, Peace and Freedom* (UK), *Dust and Fire* (USA) and *Cathal Bui* (2001).

Biographical Note

Averil Meehan was born in County Tyrone, and lives in County Donegal where she is a computing lecturer. Her writing has won awards and been short-listed in various competitions including RTE's PJ O'Connor competition for radio drama, the Allingham Festival, George A. Birmingham short story competition, Clough Writers' Annual competition, Cork Literary Review, Salopean Poetry Society, Kerry International Summer School, Athlone Festival, the Patrick McGill Summer School and the Charles Macklin Poetry competition. Her radio play *A Family Christmas* has been broadcast twice by RTE. A founder member of Errigal Writers, she took part in Poetry Ireland Introductions Series 2001, and has read her work at Cúirt and at Earagail Arts Festival.

CONTENTS

Silence

Your cries broke our sleep
the night before last.
I walked and sang
to ease you into quiet.

Last night, your pale face
lay still, your eyes stayed
closed until the darkness
dissolved into birdsong.

At the church,
I sat, I stood, I walked.
I did not speak.
I did not cry.

Back at the house
your cot does not block
the dressing-table, drawers
do not hold your clothes.

Your brown sandals
with the hole in the toe,
your teddy, your doll,
do not clutter the floor.

Was it only two nights ago
that I wished for silence?

Spiked Landing

I watch a butterfly
try to land on a thistle
and think of you.

Outstretched wings – orange
blotched with brown
edged with dark lace.

Antennae reach up
to the sun, as the scent
of roses, lupins, buddleia

wafts on warm air.
Feet stick out
at an awkward angle.

It lands on a thistle's
spiky leaf, misses
the mauve flower

that rises resplendent
from a tight fist
of purple sepals.

I tried to warn you
about barbs among blooms,
pointed out the strength

of your quiet wingspan,
showed you other flowers:
pink, yellow and red.

You blame my
distracting you
for the jags in your feet.

Haiku

Outstretched wings curve wind.
A skylark drops notes onto
woolly backs of sheep.

A crow leans wing-tips
on the wind as its shadow
surfs a sun-bright lake.

Vegetation clings
to rocks along the lakeshore
until stones blossom.

She would wait until
dusk to pump her Tilly lamp
and light its mantle.

Saturday Job

Inside the supermarket, a solid brick wall holds baskets,
each tilted and half-filled with the sweet and sour scents
of onions, celery and apples; a mosaic of red, green
and shades of earth. All around, the medley of sound
that is here every Saturday – voices, plastic bags rustle,
a metal scoop rattles among the hard-boiled sweets,
footsteps, a baby cries, a mother scolds, tills ping.

I assure a woman with a neat grey perm that these onions
are fine, wrap them in a brown paper bag, turn to see
her race towards the door. Others follow. Some run,
most saunter, chatting. The words *Bomb Scare* echo
to where I stand holding her bag of onions.
So near to lunch-time, I hope the cafes are left within
the safe zone, and pray that this time it will not rain.

Frantic waves of uniformed arms, flushed faces,
darting eyes, scurry us down the street to behind
yellow tape, where people grumble about lunch.
A shock of noise erupts up through bones and teeth.
Windows sneeze glass shards onto the pavement.
No one moves in the sudden hush until a single
scream scrapes up a rising moan of voices.

Relief at the back of my throat. No one is bleeding.
People run haphazardly through the crowd, shout
names, hug, while others tramp about with blank
eyes. A dog scurries away, tail hidden. The yellow tape
is lifted and we drift cautiously back
over broken glass. No one seems
to have an appetite for sandwiches or chips.

Outside the supermarket, a little way up the entry,
on the other side of my vegetable section,
smoke wisps upwards from a black tangled wreck.
I cannot believe how slowly I moved from here.
Inside, dust layers the hush. Vegetables and fruit
lie muddled on the floor. Empty lopsided baskets
sprout a huge bouquet of cracks up the wall.

Communication Rhythm

The dashboard glows 2.27 a.m.
and Beethoven fills the car.
You jump inside with a paper bag,
hair short, an upward flick of gel
holding a long spike at the front.

The air breathes vinegar
and the hungry smell of chips.
You dodge questions,
don't know what you did
or who you might have seen.

With the push of a button
you snap off the violins,
fill the space between us
with the electric clash of guitar,
the rapid burst of drumbeats.

Parting

A few pink roses cling to the hedge outside
but I smell only cigarette smoke and stewed tea.

If you could stand with me in this hall
beside the frosted glass in the open front door,
you would hear these neighbours and friends
chatter up the path, then hesitate, go silent
as they come inside to shake my hand.

You would laugh with me at the glowing
adjectives from the woman who hardly noticed
you at church on Sunday mornings, nod to the man
who loved to argue with you, but now opens
and closes his silent mouth, while his eyes brim.

You would acknowledge the woman
who raised her family in clothes you
brought her; the widow who found the courage
to live when you held and held her hand;
the children you talked to, now grown.

All news to me as I stand in this draughty hall
and wonder how well I really knew you.

I am handed a cup and saucer, the fine china
covered in gold swirls that you treasured
and never used, now filled up to the brim
with warm tea. It rattles in my hand, then spills.

Sand Grit

We came here on your last summer
where the dunes stop in a sheltering
cliff of sand. I watched you sleep
on a tartan rug, warm in your lemon
cardigan, quiet amid the whirling laughter
of girls in brightly coloured sun tops
and the low boom of surf.

Today, only a few figures wrapped
in hooded anoraks, move in the distance.

The wind assaults my face, jerks
my hair back as I lean forwards,
move down towards the sea.

Now I carry you safely in my head.
I do not have to slow my step, or listen
for your rising change in breathing
so that I can judge exactly when
to move more slowly.

A seagull tumbles shrieking
through grey rain-heavy sky
as I walk across tide-rippled sand,
breathe deep the salt of clearing air.

I stand at this shoreline, this end
of land, this sea you could not reach
that day, could not paddle in.

Iris

Lilac veined with purple,
an iris stands majestic among
a mess of grass. Its outer petals
reach out, then droop downwards.

A child with a patch on her glasses
stands apart from the other girls.
They all watch the rope swing round,
get ready to run as it falls, as each

in turn hops, jumps in time to the thump
of hemp on playground tarmac.
Skipping rhymes bounce around her
but she bends her head down over sandals,

unpolished leather, scuff marks on toes.
When she lifts her head, brightness
in the morning light catches her lens.
Her one visible eye is iris blue.

Moonwalk

On the week of our first date, Armstrong and Aldrin
walked on the moon. They carried air on their backs
and wore padded body suits, stripes that wrapped them
in bulk so chunky they could only walk about in jerks.

Their thick boots marked the powdery ground.
Hands, protected safe inside gloves, grasped
a flag, planted it proud, gathered soil samples,
rocks, and beamed photographs back to Earth.

That was the summer Louis Armstrong sang for us
What a Wonderful World, on your car radio.
We ate ice-cream, crunched the wafer, walked the back
beach. A crab ran sideways in front of our footsteps.

My moondress was sleeveless, striped me in pastel pink
and fuchsia as our bare feet churned a trail along the line
of tide. Sand stuck between our wet toes. We laughed,
took snapshots, and picked up abandoned bits of shell.

We strolled to the harbour, the far end of the sea wall,
where I saw only reflected rainbows in the oil
that seeped from tethered yachts. Not once
did I look up or guess at the changes in my sky.

Enamel Plate

Your enamel plate
is chipped black
and edged all around
with blue.

It goes with you to camp
as it travelled years before
in your father's kit.

You return unwashed,
smell of camp-cooking
and sweat, bring in a trail
of mud and washing.
Your cheeks gleam with fire
beneath eyes dark from exhilarated
lack of sleep.

Your father asks you
how it went.
All right, you say.

This space between us
is enamel cold,
chipped black,
edged all around
with blue.

Miscreant

The door of the classroom
bursts open, bangs back
against the wall.
He runs in late.

Brown hair tufts
argue among themselves,
his unwashed face is flushed,
triumph jostles for space
with a plea for mercy.

He is his own
morning alarm,
finds his own clothes,
makes his own breakfast,
jams his own lunch bread,
runs on his own two feet
along busy city streets
past jeering bigger boys.

Please close the door.
A smile of relief fills his cheeks
as he hurries to his chair
with shoe-laces flapping,
his world secure
until half-past three.

Luxury Coach Tour

(of 'The Troubles' in Northern Ireland)

Tourist eyes hoover up city images
matching brick and stone
to half-remembered scenes
in news bulletins that flickered,
safely insulated from their lives
by a thin layer of screen.

A man at the front microphone-guides
the cocoon of steel and stale air
as velour seats softly glide
past unyielding stone,
safely insulated from violent times
by a thin layer of peace.

The coach tour accelerates
past a woman juggling
children, bags, memories;
nothing asked,
safely insulated from contact
by a thin layer of glass.

Twenty-five historic years
scheduled before a five-star lunch.

Forgiveness

Birthday flowers on your grave,
daisy, chrysanthemum and dahlia,
echo the autumnal colours
of this giant chestnut tree.

No longer fed by parent branches,
leaves starve to red and yellow.
Hurt rusts rich and vibrant, dead leaves
cling on tight, pretending still to live.

You crushed me to autumn in my spring.
My childish leaves grew gold and brown,
not green, until I fell beneath your tree,
drowning in the rustle of leaves
blown from your branches
by life's autumnal wind.

You loved as much as you were
able, you too could not grow green.

My blooms lie on new-mown grass.
Their tawny petals burn
in end-of-summer light.

Listening

No matter how long I've been asleep
the instant you open our front door
I hear your footsteps on the tiles.

Your shoes bounce off, one at a time,
land among the geranium pots,
before you race up the stairs.

Wooden creaks and the thud of socked
feet on carpet grows louder, closer.
Your light clicks.
The quiet closing of your door,

then silence.

I snuggle down again,
this time to proper sleep.

Rescued
(for Ted Deppe)

Five years old, blond hair
tied back in bunches,
she cries for her own kitchen
where she wants to eat.

Her cup, her plate that bunny
rabbits ran around, hopped
when his fist smashed
his anger into wood.

Skipping-rope knots in her
stomach left no space then
for swallowed food, sent it
back in later bathroom-safe.

Now a nurse reads her stories,
tries to tell jokes, but the words
pull on her yo-yo, tilt her
kaleidoscope, crash her bike.

She grips a soft pink cloth,
shouts at the nurse, does not
want to stay on this *Treasure Island*
for which she has no map.

Insight

When precisely does the wind
that plays with treetops, branches,
begin tossing slates for real
as it alters into a storm to fear?

Where is the exact point
that an ocean lapping onto rocks
transforms to a wild panic crash
against their seaweed surfaces?

When did listening to your words
shift to my hearing
what you really mean?

You say you are sorry,
you will never drink again,
as you gulp down water
from a glass that trembles
with your hands.

This moment, second, aeon,
when all perspective tilts,
beats as fast
as a hummingbird's wing;

separates me from you
by a line as fine
as silkworm thread,
a space as wide and deep
as the red clay
of a cactus-studded canyon.

Flowers

When I ask about the war,
It was fine, you tell me,
then talk of the weather,
or the price of cigarettes.

You still jolt awake at dawn,
check around the room
to count how many of the men
who stood beside you in khaki,
tanned under a hot foreign sun,
now lie still on their billet,
soaked red by an assassin's visit.

You see only your wife's curls,
hear her breathing, as light filters
through pink satin curtains
splattered with clumps of roses.

These flowers hang on guard all night,
keep back snipers and their bullets
while you try to get some sleep
under the curtains' matching bedspread,
drowning in a pool of pink petals.

New Baby

I watch you sleep in your glass cot,
legs and arms still folded. One day old,
too small to stretch or find its edges.

I wait for you to wake, ready to lift the warm
burrowing hug of you; place you across
the soft cuddle of my dressing gown,

pink candlewick, pretty-girl-safe colour;
watch you fold arms around the mound
you left behind just yesterday, the bump

that still holds your place, that you love to lie
along, clinging to touch and sounds you know.
Have you learned too much from me?

You push out one leg, then the other,
as your fingers and hands stroke air
and eyes open in dark blue surprise at light.

Daughter of Seventeen

A fledgling with all her feathers
totters at her edge of the nest,
peeps down the steep cliff face,

looks out across the grey
and white swirls that drift past,
her claws buried in soft straw.

You rush around the house,
your voice high with excitement,
cheeks flushed, your eyes bright.

You re-read your college prospectus,
worry about the width of hem
on your jeans, wonder if you should

wear your hair tied up or loose,
insist you get new runners, fret
about your weight, invisible spots.

Soon you will fly, free
to make your own mistakes.
Choking on advice, all I can do

is applaud when you tumble down
through cloud-patterned air,
rocked by turbulence until

you learn to soar on the breeze,
wave proud, as I stand
on straw, damp with missing.

Birthday Sheep

You will be twenty years old this week
and I want to give you sheep.

Whole flocks of them; noisy, jostling
bodies that will hem in your legs and keep
you standing on the ground, on safe soil –
a carpet of thick woollen backs to warm
your fingers as you stroke along them.

When you were nine and one of your pet
lambs died, I could not soften the hard jut
of your chin, its upward tilt to hold back
tears, could not ease the cut on your lip
where teeth pressed sharp through skin.

I want to take wool from these sheep
and knit it around you in blackberry stitch,
moss stitch, honeycomb and basketweave,
so the cold wind won't bite your ears
to a raw red, so your body is hug-warm,
so your feet step only in soft.

But my stitches cannot keep you safe.
For this birthday, I've chosen cotton,
shop-bought, crisp black denim to match
your black boots and your dark hair, once
a mass of curls, now cut to a No. 1 sheen.

Beyond the Waves

I think of you as I stand at this window. The ocean below me
is strewn with dark rocks that fuse with blue-green
water as it swells up, around and over them, then drops
back, leaves them clinging on to layers of white foam.

Every weekend for months you brought me with you, to watch
while you stepped onto raised velvet-lined circular platforms,
tried on wedding dress after dress, your face animated
as you worried about the position of sequins, what fabric

to choose. Was taffeta too stiff? Would silk crease? Was white
too harsh against the sallow warmth of your skin? Anxious
about overdoing lacy frills, you wonder if a seam should lie
on or below your waist, how long your train should be.

My own mother was married in a linen suit with sleeves
that reached her elbows, two roses with ferns on her lapel.
She smiled for the camera with your dark eyes,
sure then that her future would be different.

Her hair was thicker than yours, curled up and out from her
face, and held her wedding hat like an aura around her.
You cannot decide on what veil to choose, but are sure that
fine net, framed with a diamanté tiara is all your head needs.

I bend down, lift one stone up, feel it smooth and snug in my
palm. I swing my arm, then let it go, up, out, to arc beyond
the suck-back that rattles pebbles at my feet, further than
breaking waves. It slips with a splash into the calmer deep.

Twenty-four Seven

Neat grey curls, perm-box perfect,
handbag clutched tight on knees,
lips pressed firm together, chin tilted
up, her eyes stare to the left of the stage.

He sits beside her and chain smokes.
Strands of hair cross his shiny dome.
His legs are crossed, back is straight
as his body faces away to the right.

Lights flash, fireworks blast into a night sky.
On stage Tina Turner sings her life, radiates
energy from a short white dress, dances
on amazing legs and impossible heels.

We leap, jump and bounce to the beat
that vibrates the molecules of air,
ricochets onto trampled grass, against metal
stands, up through concrete and wooden seats.

Everyone is on their feet, arms waving,
shouting her tune. All except this couple
who stay seated and still, not touching,
totally absorbed in their own silent row.

Morning After the Wedding

It is too early in the day
and too late in the year for heat.
The hedge clings to clusters
of reddening berries and
brown leaves dried in curls.

Earlier in the year, this hedge
blossomed into creamy spikes,
the colour of the dress you wore
yesterday, long and flowing,
pearls stitched along the seams.

Now the sun hangs too low,
barely skims the horizon,
a token presence of light
that pushes sideways out
from grey clouds overhead.

Up through the bare branches,
long sycamore stems hold out
black tight buds that reach
skywards with a growth
that is faster than hedge speed.

You will open vibrant leaves
in spring, but will never sit again
with me on Saturday mornings,
wearing only your pyjamas,
as we chat about our week.

Your Kitchen Floor

is a draught-board of blue and yellow,
vinyl that refuses to stay stuck down.
You step from tile to tile as if everything
is fine, then trip on a newly raised edge,

arms flapping with the jolt, only just
managing to stay upright. You talk
about new surfaces; soft carpet, warm
underfoot of cork, or the strength

of quarry tiles, able for your trek across
this room. When a square of concrete,
pale, dry and colourless, is exposed,
you reach fast for your tub of glue.

You blame the steam, the tread of feet,
poor quality cement; buy stronger adhesive;
apply it in zig-zag patterns over backs of tiles;
stick down hard, leap, jump, stamp them down.

Tiles now hold at their centre, but the edges
escape and corners curl up, then snap. Black
uneven lines mark new patches, refuse to erase
under breathless scrubbing, will not lie flat.

You cover the worst areas with off-cuts
of carpet, orange swirls on beige and brown.
You move these about, search for the best position
to hide the disintegration under your feet.

No Recovery

The nurse who should be too busy
finds time to sit us down
and explain. For the first time
the language I've used since birth
makes less sense than the Latin
declensions I once struggled with.

I sit beside you, hold your hand,
while you hide among tubes.

A green light moves jagged
lines across a monitor. Your breaths
keep perfect time with the whisper
from some machine. Behind me
there is a swish of curtain; soft
footsteps move over a polished
floor. A door closes.

My shoes are covered in sterile
white cloth. A theatre gown
hides my new red dress.
A bleached cap covers hair
that I washed until it shone for you.

No chance of stray germs escaping
into this intensive quiet,

but if you were able to open
your eyes, how would you know
it was me in this sterile disguise?

Yellow

is the colour of the sun at the top
of every painting I brought home to you,
a round bright ball suspended in blue
and surrounded by thick rays – scenes
you sellotaped to walls, fridges, doors;

the colour of the jumper you knitted for me,
thick stitches that matted together after a first
wash into an itchy mess that kept me warm;
the colour of the catalogue dress you cut back
on food to buy, long ties around the waist,

neat collar, ruched bodice with white embroidery
that I stained dark blackberry-purple,
snagging its shine with wild rose thorns,
worn with a pretty-girl bonnet, tied
in a choking bow under my chin;

the colour of crocus spears that pushed aside clay
and snow to rise into the cold air of late winter,
brightness that followed us on every house move,
lined the path from gate to our front door
with glow amid the grey and umber foliage;

the colour of the grown-up bed-jacket you knitted
for me when you felt the chill around *your* shoulders
as you read in bed. I take it now from the airing
cupboard, feel its cheerful soft, see even rows
of stitches made with your arthritic fingers;

the colour of the flowers you loved –
chrysanthemums, canary bird daisies,
yellow asters, and roses, always roses;
the colour of blooms I lay on your grave.

Their Heart Attack

A heart attack strengthens his will-power
to reject battered fish, chips in curry sauce;
to endure, complaining, the green and red
patterns that now landscape his plate,
while he pats with pride a leather belt
once hidden by his stomach overhang.

His wife sleepwalks through a tired haze
to feed sick-visiting family and friends,
deflects their bullets of blame, while she
listens through days – forced, idle, long –
as he watches all she is doing wrong.

Slipper-shod on eggshells, his children
circle his temper, no longer confined
inside his hangover. Money leaks
to thinner new clothes, smart suits,
as their bicycle dreams evaporate.

Woman Eats Pig's Feet

(after a painting by Pauline Bewick)

I was ready to eat with you. I pulled my hair back
so hard my eyes slanted; wound my hair on rollers
to curl it down my back; dressed up in swirling blue
fabric stamped with gold leaves; shaded my eyes
pale blue to match my collar; revealed curves
at the top of my breasts. But you did not come.

So I turn my back on the window that looks out
over the chimney pots, the glass dome, to a sky
that holds pigeons. I lean my elbows on the table
and read Beckett's love songs as I eat alone.

I do not notice that my teeth caress a raw
pig's foot until they clash on trotter bone.

Wood

He was three when he first grabbed
a hammer and nails, held out
proudly his achievement.

Since then he has built trailers
for bikes, doghouses, fences,
tables for birds, bookcases, chairs,
as the wood around his home
grew under his hands.

Now, out of his first car he lifts
a bootful of wooden planks,
lays them gently on the garage floor.

Every spare second he goes there.
His short, dark hair freckled
with sawdust; eyes intent;
checked sleeves rolled up;
jeans with a hole on the thigh
worn by the duress of planks;
pencil behind his ear.

He lifts, marks wood laid along
the workbench he designed, constantly
compares with lengths pulled
from his vibrant green tape-measure.

The silence shatters as saw dictates
to wood, chisel-flakes sliver,
and hammer jolts crash down.

School days left behind. Years
when his ear was pulled so hard
he was lifted clear from his seat,
all because he could not nail
his letters into words.
Called *Stupid* because he had
no spirit level then, could not align
historic names with dates.

Years he sat in desks
he could have made.

Hot and Cold

Huddled against the curve of night, we watch
orange flames chase wisps of smoke as they rise
out of the bedroom window, up and over
the roof. A shattering blast spits glass
onto the concrete yard below. A sudden
surge of black smoke whirls out – dense swirls

punctured by flames that curl upwards
over cracking slates. Firemen yell, water
hisses, splatters the air with noise not loud
enough to cover a daughter's gentle sobs.
We stand as close to heat as we can bear.
Teeth clattering, we shiver, and long for cold.

Next morning the sun shines on quiet.
I must breathe shallow, still choke on smoke-laden
stink, as I look and look. Up where the roof
used to angle, is a space filled only
with sky. When this numbness fades I will
try to be thankful my boys lost only their room.

A wet nose touches my hand. The dog pushes
against my leg, his tail down, eyes asking,
asking. I have no answers, stand as close
as I dare to a black gap that was once my door.
Unable to make myself enter, I can only stare.
Teeth clattering I shiver, and long for warm.

Wide Awake Child

When voices rise in anger
he snuggles down into the safe
warm shell of his bed.

Images of a school trip
light up his darkness:
fish that swam brightly
on the far side of glass;
a startled turtle that hid
head and limbs, then floated
down to wait for calm.

His mother's silence
blasts the room – fear
turned up full volume.

A door slams. Her sobs
edge the quiet just within
reach of his hearing.

He thinks of soft fur, a cat
on his knee, purring trust.

Echoes

A girl child, not two, lies dead
in disbelieving arms.
One moment – all it takes
to move from finding ways to cope
with sleepless nights, crying long,
to living silent endless days.

Other children cannot fill
this empty desolating void.
But other children will not die.
Secure, they stay in gardens
where a locked gate guards
lonely protected play.

Safeness stirred into their milky
drinks, echoed with their nursery
rhymes, until they are forced to learn
how to prise a space for self,
move out from under the crush
of their parents' suffocating care.

Watching Wimbledon

I have earned the right to breathe this air,
worked years for it, a whole lifetime.

A good baby who seldom cried,
quiet child who swallowed questions,
I learned to be a lady – enjoy tea
instead of beer, sit with legs together,
wear skirts below my knee, never open
blouses below button number two;

always chose serious browns, greys
or pastels – colour bleached of passion;
learned a hundred ways to talk about
the weather; pulled cheeks tight
over longing; carved lips into smiles;
cut hair short in a careful perm;
rejected gaudy silver for elegant pearl.

Is this my reward? To sit here, in this
damn hard chair, watch those skits of girls,
racquets in hand, bent over in white dresses
far too short to cover frilly pants, deep
slashed tops that burst with cleavage?

They break every rule, yet still they breathe
with ease, show no sign of pain, while
I wheeze hard, know the air I grab gets thinner,
more useless, with every watching gasp.

Bare

You sit on a mustard-leather armchair at your solid-fuel hearth.
Heat hides behind smoke-darkened glass, leaks a faint sulphur
stink. A cigarette leans sideways between your fingers. Smoke

spirals while a cup of cooling tea waits on the fender at your feet.
Your eyes crinkle up and you remember summer; when brown
bears covered in thick fur stood taller than a man's span to pad

over pine needles, huge paws clawed at trunks, left scars oozing
resin. A dragonfly had its legs stuck there; long, iridescent
wings struggled, caught slivers of rainbow light. When your bears

stepped on branches, cracking startled the red deer that nibbled
on celandine, so they ran crashing through the forest. Wood
pigeons and doves flapped upwards into a crescendo of flight.

Have you forgotten that I too was there in that past? I remember
autumn; grey rocks barely covered with brown grass,
end-of-season ferns purpled only with a few speckles of heather.

Leave-taking

You followed your brothers up trees,
got stuck there, unable to climb down.
Your childhood was spent outside
as much as you were allowed, scented
with lilac and the stink from the cowshed.

You worked on a hospital ward
like this one; wore white, delivered babies,
washed mothers, changed bed-linen,
kept your corners neat, held the hand
of a dying child all night. He lived.

You loved to sit by the range – a mug of tea
in your hand, and when the breadman came,
a sugar-filled bun – talking of the times
you helped your father count his sheep.

You would not talk about your dead baby –
the one in the black-and-white photograph
hidden inside your wardrobe, smiling
in a black-and-white pram with large wheels.

You do not talk now, lie tucked in with neat
hospital corners. Nurses wash you, tubes
nourish, while I hold and hold your hand.

You Did Not Name Me

You learned that you carried me
when autumn stained the bracken purple.

You talked to me, called me *Heather*,
the hardy plant that grows on acid soil,
able to flourish on a thin wedge of black
clay trapped behind an outcrop of rock.

You believed the doctors when they said
you would not survive my birth.
Waited between starched sheets.
Thought about your loved dead father.
He held your hand, walked you over hills
to count and check his sheep, as you both
pushed upwards through the heather.

My aunt could not feel me kick or move.
You did not mention *Heather*, instead
asked her to choose my name.

You wanted me to root in scraps of acid
clay, caught behind jutting stone.
You wanted me to blaze across barren hilltops.
You wanted me to flourish purple.

Your gift was not to name me.

Unlaced

In all the years I knew you, you wore
sensible shoes, brown or navy laced-up
for control, safe low heels.

From under your stairs I take out bags,
reach through dark, breathe air stale
with dust, push past cobwebs and books.

At the back, the thin point
of wedge where the stairs begin
to rise, I pull free a cardboard box.

Inside is a plastic bag stuffed
with dank tissue and in it I discover
a pair of shoes, your exact size.

White leather and snakeskin with open
toes, fine straps around your ankles,
curved in a high arch over the heel.

I push away webs to see you then,
before you lost your first-born child
and ran foot-long into sorrow's wall.

These would have swayed your legs,
drawn everyone's eye as you walked.

Surviving Motherhood

I have two toothbrushes.
The best one mocks me,
dripping black oil.

My protests meet amazement:
But it was great for cleaning
my radio-control car!

I have one toothbrush that smiles
blue hairs from scrubbing
the stain on a daughter's jumper.

My exasperation meets anger
that I dare to challenge
the age-old law of motherhood:

what's theirs is theirs
and what's mine
is theirs as well.

I have a new toothbrush,
prisoner in my underwear
drawer, on parole

to the bathroom,
guarded and never
left alone.

Sodden Scents

You come out, join me on the damp wicker.
In the steaming warmth the air feels washed fresh.
The smell of spearmint flows from around
the filled-in well and the lawn is transformed

from brown and beige to olive, spiked
all over with dabs of vibrant green.
Birds celebrate in trees behind us. All along
the red rooftops, short chirps, longer notes,

then a flapping intensifies around the chimney.
A van stops on the lane outside. French
voices sing an exchange that drowns
the hum of cars from the far, unseen road.

The Christmas tree has a faint whiff of pine,
is decorated with impossibly large drops
of water that cling to each needle
and reflect the grey sky above us.

The willow branches arch, flow and dip.
Periwinkle plays round pots, hugs the house.
Vines float along the top of the wall, held
there by stems that rise from the herb bed.

Lavender, parched for weeks, lies sodden,
scents the air, mingles with the whiff of sage;
soft furry leaves edged with pale gold.
As we sit together your hand touches mine.

Singing Loud

The sound is turned up high.
The Royal Philharmonic Orchestra
plays hide-and-seek with melodies
that dart around my orange sofas
and the tweed-covered chair.

Violins reverberate from behind
tapestries of country scenes,
over the mirror
to bounce off ceiling boards.

I, who cannot hold a tune
anywhere but in my head,
chase these notes, free
the silence of the good little girl
who listened to voices –
to hush, to shush, to never be.

I belt out *Up Where We Belong*
and *Any Dream Will Do*.

Shipwrecked

Three children wait,
television their focus

of nonchalant pretence,
as his lateness tightens
the constricting band
that sharpens listening.

Long gap from his car's
jerking stop to door handle's
rattle – ignored. They sit
very still, eyes on the set.

The outside door flies in.
He navigates the rolling waves
from cooker to cupboard,
grasps at the door frame.

Without a chart he cannot
find his chair, flounders
on the carpet – the desert
island of their childhood.

Rock Climb

I sit on the edge of a sheer slice of hill,
secured by heavy twine to solid stone,
peer down as I lower the rope that you
tie securely to the D-ring on your waist.

I cheer as you rise, slowly, foothold
by foothold, balance on a horizontal wedge,
reach for a fissure hardly wide enough
to let your fingers gain sufficient grasp.

I catch glimpses of cropped hair, your arms
outstretched, legs longer now, to reach
further, higher, wider, as the distance
between us closes. The depth of your fall

to ground, if your fingers should ever
slip, makes me spin. My own rope
is ready, winds shorter, tighter round
my anchor boulder as you slowly rise.

First I see your fingers, then elbows.
One leg goes sideways, your knee grips,
arms press down hard as you throw your
whole self up to land beside me and grin.

Picnic

You drove us along the country roads
all packed in together in an old black car.

We ran through bluebells, ducked under
cool branches, breathed the damp green
smell of pine flavoured with wild garlic,
gathered on a tartan rug to eat
cold sausages sliced in bread.

When life ruffles I return there,
run on sandalled feet through bluebells,
collect pine cones in cool shade,
eat with fresh-air appetite, and shout
loud through fir-tree branches.

Uses of Light

It filters through blinds says his widow
with no one to hold her as people gather round.

It shows us fields of barley growing tall say the crows
with no one to shoot as we gather his grain.

It shines on crowds standing in black says his brother
with no one talking as he gathers a fistful of earth.

It finds me with torch beam says his collie dog
but no one will help me to gather him back.

It finds us stranded on cliff-tops say his sheep
and no one knows we are here gathering grass.

It sprouts the spuds that he planted say his children
but no one will sit on his chair as we gather to eat.

Perennial

Your ditch was green, lined with buttercups
and overlooked by splashes of wild rose.
Years later I return along your country road,
half expect a ruin, see instead a rainbow
of colour growing along the base of your hedge.

A wire fence once guarded pinks and hollyhocks
in a hen-safe rectangle in your yard.
These are gone but along the house base
are a line of gaudy annuals, one-season colour
you never would have planted.

I am surprised by the gentle breath of smoke
that oozes upwards into the cloud-filled sky
from the far chimney set on dark grey tin.
Your small windows that I once peeped from
are dark squares set in thick stone.

Your green door lies ajar to only shadow,
yet I still see you standing there; still smell
buttermilk while you hand me bronze-crusted
scone bread, butter melting; still feel warmth
from between the metal bars of your turf range.

Landlocked

I wake early on this, my landmark birthday, walk around
the lake, enjoy the early morning freshness, wrapped up
tightly in my scarf, jacket, boots and knitted hat.

The lake is steel-grey, looks as hard as plate. Tiny
ripples move across the surface like dents left by hammer
blows on a thin metal sheet. All around its seaward side

is a wall of boulders: huge stones are piled high with a duvet
of grass tucked over them, patterned with dandelion and clover.
I climb until a rush of cold air pushes at me, slaps my face.

Below is the chopped-up green-blue of open ocean,
magnolia splashes where sea water catches the rocks.
I turn to watch clouds of midges hover over the lake

until a trout leaps up into the air, splashes back, breaks
the surface calm for a moment before ripples settle
and water reflects only sky. I think back over my life,

times when a wall of stones on my seaward side seemed so high
I lived as if I were a lake; forgot I was really an ocean;
forgot about motion; forgot about reaching deep down

to my sea bed. The clouds part and early sun brightens
the green beneath my feet. I loosen my scarf, unzip
my jacket, pull off my hat, feel the breeze move my hair,

see the brine splashing at black chunks of granite.
Lines of light reach from a widening chink of sky down
to the Atlantic, white waves on vivid cobalt.

Lab Report

A white-coated expert
diligently watches
the laboratory rat
in its cage, notes down
with care its behaviour
and any deviation.

The rat eats the food
it is given, runs around
its exercise wheel.
That it doesn't do
much else is noted.
The cage bars
don't get a mention.

When the rat sits still
the logbook records
vacant contentment,
not the rat's mind-pictures
as it keeps up
with world events,

skimming news printed
on the cage's paper lining.

Garments

I remember you sitting for hours
as your swollen finger joints moved
fast, pulled aran wool over, around,
back and through needles that clicked
out intricate patterns onto your lap.

Your own jumper and skirt hid under
brown nylon: large orange roses grew over
a housecoat, taken off only when the front
doorbell chimed, your fingers combing
hair as you went through the hall.

Now I learn that once you wore elegant
hats, that you were seen only in the latest
fashion, liked fitted dresses worn with high-heeled
shoes or boots, that you danced
all night and that you laughed out loud.

Dice

A simple test, they said.
You could be home by evening.

When your phone does not answer
in the rush up to Christmas, I talk myself
into believing that you are busy.

When your presents arrive
at nine in the morning
with your husband and three young sons,
even before I see his face, I know.

I sit stunned, hear disjointed words
that snag on the fir tree, hang there suspended
among red glass balls and golden angels
while your children help mine to tear open
the bright parcels you wrapped so neatly.

Years ago you sat beside me in school.
Now each of your children share
a classroom with one of mine.
I watch them shake the dice,
move across the board, your gift to them.

We landed on many squares together:
science lab where we sat close enough
to pass each other notes; the student flat
where we learned to cook toast and beans;

factory where we spent a summer making
toys. If my legs would take me, I could see
your house from my landing window.

Open your present, Mammy, excited voices plead.
I see blurred faces, shake my head. Not yet.

Birthday Tune

Today would have been your birthday.
Barley stubble scuffles against my boots.
The dog races, nose down, zig-zagging
over invisible paths across the field.

Small dark birds sit on parallel electric
wires, their beaks all pointing south.
Enough leaves have autumned
for the hedge to show its branches.

There are blackberries still, scarcer now
and smaller. The birds fly off in a flapping
dotted arc as wind keens a tune on the wires.
Brown-edged leaves rustle deeper notes.

Roberta

Her eyes
were navy blue.
Most baby   eyes
start off   that way,
then change   or   lighten,
but hers   stayed dark
as if she   knew that
she would never
grow old.

Second Baby
(to my first born)

Her head sleeps in reflected moonlight
as her tiny body gently falls and rises
behind the wooden bars of your cot,
where she lies on no-wrinkles cotton.

No cries shatter the long darkness.
Instead she rests still, does not scream
as you did, with your eyes and fists
screwed up tight with your need of me.

She stays wrapped, hug-tight, making
gentle lip noises as she dreams, in your
blanket, lying in your space, where you
should be warm, should be growing,